Love Notes

Mark Anthony

*"Time tells us
if it's love."*

Follow Mark Anthony on Instagram: @markanthonypoet

Publisher's Note: This is a work of poetry. Names, characters, places, and incidents are the product of the author's life, love, and inspiration.

Book Layout © 2015 BookDesignTemplates.com

Love Notes/ Mark Anthony. -- 1st ed.
ISBN 9781721728589

For my one and only Bird,
the light and love
of my life.

4

Contents:

Part One

Part 2

Part 1. Advice for the Young at Heart

The Muse

She wanted to know
why I loved her,
so I told her
there are so many reasons
it would fill a book,
and so she asked me
to start writing,
and I haven't stopped
writing since.

The Depth of You

Poetry,
my dear,
reminds us
it's okay
to be
ourselves,
even when
the rest
of the world
tells us
it isn't.

Welcome Back Home

The breakup was over;
she wiped her tears,
and felt something
peaceful inside,
as if it was all
meant to be.

She felt the stars
glittering in the sky,
and the wind
whispering upon her face.

Everything was as beautiful
as it was before them;

And for the first time
in a very long time,
she felt truly alive.

She was falling in love
with herself again,
as if she were
a beautiful stranger.

Essential

Let go of the old lies
you keep telling yourself
in the dark,
those tired whispers
the world told you to believe
when you were young;

you're creating the universe
right now,
with either love or fear,
passion or poison;

So love yourself
as you would love to be loved,
and burn the rest
like a pile of old letters
written by somebody
who never really knew you.

Reminders

You deserve
a true love.

A love who
tells you
they care;

A love who
listens
when
you speak.

A love who
chooses you
above
the rest.

Soul Work

Finding your soulmate
isn't so much about fate
or destiny,
as it is about patience
and doing your best
to become
the kind of person
you want
your soulmate
to meet
when they
walk
into the room.

Twin Flames

You won't meet
your soulmate
until
you're both
ready
to say hello
to forever.

Strength & Courage

If you get back
with them
out of weakness,
and desperation,
they will not
respect you,
nor themselves;

They will
resent you
for not having
the courage
to move on;

because
love,
if anything,
is doing
the right thing,
even when it's hard.

Simplicity

She wants the kind of love
that lets go of the past,
lives in the present,
and makes plans for the future.

Love Conquers All

You deserve the best
in this world, my dear,
and your love
is bigger
than their hate,
because your smile
is the reason
the universe
exists.

Daily Reminders

You're important,
You're deserving,
You're worth it,
You're beautiful,
You're strong,
You're perfect as you are,
You're rare,
You're real,
You're you.

The Little Things

Don't forget
to appreciate
all the little things
about her
that you love:
her smile,
her laughter,
her voice,
the sweet songs
she sings
in the shower
just before
she walks
into the bedroom
to take
your breath away.

Patience

I know what it feels like
to be single,
to have to wait and wonder
when love will arrive
at your door.

But even then
I knew
I would never settle
for anyone less
than you.

Amour

Love is a language
spoken in a foreign land
and the longer you live there,
the easier it is to understand.

Letting Go

Saying goodbye
to somebody
who
is not right
for you
is a greater
act of love
than staying
and saying
nothing
at all.

Trust

has a breaking point,
and sometimes
it's better
to pick up the pieces
and move on,
than pretending
to fix
something
that can't be
put back together.

Emotions

aren't something
to be feared,
but a sign
that you're alive,
and trying;

Numbness
is a far far more dangerous
thing.

The Lesson

Most
happy
endings
began
after
a
terrible
goodbye.

The Date

It's time
to start dating
yourself again,
and to remember
how okay you were
before you met them,
and that you're still
the same beautiful badass
you've always been.

Truth & Consequences

After he had broke
his word,
he broke his heart,
and had only silence
and tears
to hold on to her,
and it was not enough
to keep them
together,
or bring back
what was already gone.

Masterpiece

Every path
to mending
a broken heart,
begins with a desire
to turn the chaos
of your life
into a work of art;

So find a way
to paint
yourself
whole again,
unto you can see
the big picture
and the beauty
of
how it all
worked out
for the best.

The One

You've always been
more than enough,
my dear;

you just needed
to find the one
who could
see it.

Les Liaisons Dangereuses

If you begin a relationship
based on seduction
instead of sincerity,
whatever is left unspoken
when you were playing games,
will be the very words
that break you up
in the end.

Her Love Lives

in the laughter of children,
and in the beauty of pouring rain;

Her love lives in the landscapes
of rural towns,
and in the neon promises
of the city;

Her love lives
in the dreams of angels,
and in the confusion
of human beings on earth.

And she's waiting
for you to find her,
and to remember
all the beautiful places
there
are
to
fall
in
love.

This Too Shall Pass

One day
all the pain
you felt
will no longer matter,
because it will be
just a memory
of one day
when it hurt,
and next day
when it didn't.

Actions Greater Than Words

The most important poetry
I write
is not with a pen,
but in the way
I treat her.

Never Settle For Less

A good heart
deserves
a good home.

Your patience
will be rewarded
with a love
that's true.

Act Boldly

Find the courage
in your heart
to do what's right,
and great forces
will always come
to your assistance.

Timing

If you haven't found
the love of your life yet,
it doesn't mean
they are not out there.

It just means
the time isn't yet right.

And,
timing in love
is everything.

Sabotage

If they don't deserve you,
part of them knows it,
and they will sabotage
the relationship
because they lack
the courage
to say goodbye.

Take this
as the best blessing
they could give,
and move on
to find
the one
who deserves
somebody
as beautiful
and rare
as you.

The Siren's Song

She walked along the beach
letting the warm water
spill over her feet and ankles,
and just the kiss of the ocean
and the touch of the sand,
made her feel
as seductive as a siren
torn between two lovers,
one calling from the land,
the other calling from the sea.

Self-Confidence

You are worth more
than you give
yourself credit for;

Think back
on all the badass
things you've done,
and remember
that was you
who did that,
and it is you
who can
do it
again.

Remember

We all have days
when we feel down
and defeated,
days when it feels
like the world
has turned its back;

Remember:

you are not alone.

Remember:

the sun is still shining
and just waiting
for you
to feel it
again.

Tips For Lasting Love

Show them you care,
with actions and with words.

Be true to your word.

Admit when you're wrong.

Forgive them when they're wrong.

Remember to be spontaneous,
and full of laughter.

Remember time flies,
and that love is a blessing.

Repeat.

Often.

Wait For It

My dear,
true love only comes
once in a lifetime,
so be patient,
and trust
that whoever it is,
they
will be worth
the wait.

How To Find True Love

Find yourself first,
what you love,
what turns you on,
and how to be at peace;

Then, never settle
for anyone
who doesn't compliment you,
and give you even more
of what
you already have.

A Question

If they don't know
what they want in life,
how can they know
if they want you?

She

She's not broken,
but beautiful;

She's savage
elegance.

She's wild
and
wonderful.

She's fierce,
and forever.

And she
is a poem
about,

You.

Right Now

the love of your life
is searching for you,
without knowing
your name,
but already knowing
the secret yearning
of your
heart.

Commitment

I'm committed to her,
which means she can trust me
to stay with her,
through good times and bad.

It means when everybody else
has gone away,
she can count on me
to be one who stays.

The Way to Love

When you find the right person,
it will be an end to games,
and the beginning of sincerity,
and vulnerability,
and the laughter
that is born of trust
and innocence.

It will be the beginning
of letting go of old fears,
and learning to embrace
the unknown
with the faith of a frozen flower
waiting for Spring;

It will be sailing off
into an uncharted land,
where the only thing
you will know for certain,
is that this is the way to love.

He Should Know

My dear,
don't let him tell you,
you're anything less
than everything
he's ever dreamed of.

The Irony

If you put in more effort
than they deserve,
they won't appreciate it,
and are more likely
to lose respect for you
for not being brave enough
to call them on it.

Just Listen

If he doesn't
listen to you,
he doesn't know
what your heart
is saying,
so how
can this be love?

True Love

There is nothing wrong
with longing for true love,
as long as you realize
it has to begin
with truly loving
yourself.

Forever

begins
when
you
meet
the
right
person
at
the
right
time.

Heart

She picked up the pieces
of her broken heart,
and built it into something
even more beautiful.

True Happiness

comes from embracing
everything about ourselves
we've been hiding
from the world,
and saying,
"This is who I am,"
without the need
for apology
or applause.

True Romance

is what happens
when we let go
of expectations,
and kiss
the moment
as it
flies.

Catch

She's a good woman
with a wild heart
and a loyal soul,
so love her
like she deserves,
and hold on to her
forever.

Love is Always Free

When I let
my heart
go free,
it always
flies back
to her.

Eyes of Love

She admired people
like the flowers
in her garden,
each one
holding
their own
unique
beauty,
color,
and story.

The Secret

The secret is to never lose sight
of each other,
and to remember that what brought you
together in the first place,
is why you are still together now;

The secret is to listen and learn
from each other,
and to know each of you
has secret wounds
that take time to heal.

The secret is to know love
is always a journey,
and never a destination.

Love is never just a kiss,
but all the reasons
we move closer.

The Journey

Broken hearted girls
become women warriors
who can change the world.

Tempus Fugit

If you're on the right path,
you will know it
by the effortlessness
of your steps,
the beauty of your surroundings,
and the lack of hurry
you feel
to get to the end.

Part 2.   In Dreams Begin Realities

Somewhere

between her dreams
and her fears,
she made the choices
that turned her
into the hero
of her own story.

The Paradox

Love is making
plans for tomorrow,
while living
in the moment
where everything
seems to happen
in ways
you never
could
have
planned.

Trust

And if you should
ever fall,
I will catch you,
and remind you
that you can fly.

The Courage to be Yourself

She always feared
being too much
for them;
too loud,
too passionate,
too strong,
but the truth is,
these are exactly
the qualities
that attracted me to her,
and what separated her
from the rest.

Carpe Diem

Don't let anybody tell you
you're small or insignificant
because you are life itself
searching for sunlight.

You are a flower
a bird,
an ocean,
an earthquake,
a poem being recited
by the earth.

It trembles
when you tremble,
and breathes
when you breathe,
and loves when you love,
so what are you waiting for?

This moment is all you have,
and that is more than enough time
to break the universe into song.

Real Magic

True love
doesn't vanish
when times
get tough;

it shines
all the way
through.

Star Gazing

Just think
before we met
we were both looking
at the same stars,
and dreaming of the same love.

A Madness Like No Other

You have
to be
a
        little crazy
in love,

because
      love
is so much more
than
logical,

so much more
than

one
          simple
  reason.

Done

She finally found
the courage
to say
goodbye to maybes.

End Game

In the end,
she needed
so little
to be happy:

sunlight
upon the water,
and his hand
in hers.

Courageously

To be open
and vulnerable
to the world
is the only way
to receive
all its gifts.

Love Song

I remember
listening to music
and feeling like
we were every love song
ever written.
but the yearning
I felt for her then
is not the same
as it is now,
because it
has grown deeper
with time;

When she is absent,
it is simply my soul
longing for my soul:

The longing for
a familiar voice
to untangle me
from the petty darkness.

Each Day

with her,
I taste
a little more
of forever.

The Dreamers

In the end she saw
there were only a precious few
who stayed in place
long enough to listen,
and fewer still
who got the puzzle of her soul.

And so she longed
for these people always,
the ones
who made her feel less alone.

The ones you have only
to meet once,
and you feel as if
you're know them
for a lifetime.

Longing

It happens when you least expect it,
and you can't force it.

Yet there is something beautiful
about its ache,
a simple pleasure that comes
when you realize
somebody
has touched your soul
so deeply
it hurts
to want
to see
them
again.

The Perfection Paradox

I accept her flaws,
and she accepts mine,
and it works out
to perfection.

Relationships

Some
relationships
teach us
what we
don't want;

Some
relationships
teach us,
we can have
it all.

Facts

You deserve
somebody
who doesn't
have to make you
a priority
in their life,
because
you are
their life.

Your Smile

reminds me
what happiness
looks like.

Insomnia

There are nights without you
when I can't sleep;
as if with fever,
my body won't rest
without your cool waist
resting against mine,
like moonlight upon the sea.

Open Your Eyes

Don't think for a moment
you don't deserve everything
your heart desires,
for you are made of stardust
and miracles,
and everything is already
inside you,
perfect as it is;

It is just waiting for you
to close your eyes
and see it.

I'm Yours

I love the tenderness
she gives to me,
the way she doesn't judge
my appearance
or my pain,
the way she kisses me,
and accepts me,
and steals me
back from the world,
and into her arms.

Love Story

There are no miracles
to match the gift you give me
when you walk into a room,
and smile.

Every day
the light of the universe
shines through you
like an exquisite flower,
radiating treasure
beyond measure.

The days pass
like old newspapers,
so let our love
be the news
that stays news,
and our story
the love story
that always
stays true.

Soul

What a beautiful thing
it is to find somebody
who is both strong and soft,
somebody who can match
the texture of your soul.

How to Weather a Storm

Feelings in a relationship
come and go like clouds,
so be patient,
and wait for the calm
after the storm.

Then speak from your heart,
not your fear.

The Bedroom Window

She kissed me sweetly
beneath a tangerine sun,
and her eyes had the color of youth,
and the wind kissed her skin
and her body
was like fire in my hands,
and through the window,
all the clocks
stopped chiming
and the traffic stopped
moving,
leaving us
to disappear
into into the infinity
of each other's arms.

The Most Beautiful People

The most beautiful people
I know
live life in the moment;

They make time for others,
and appreciate everything
they've been given.

They have no need
for piles of silver and gold
because they already have
the sun and the moon.

Heart Work

And should you
ever feel broken,
know that I am here
to help you find the pieces
and put them back
where they belong.

The Gift

Since you've entered my life,
every day feels right.

I do not wander
without without direction
or purpose.

Since you've entered my life,
I know I have found the secret
I've always searched for,
and the one I will always love.

Gratitude

She's brave and beautiful,
fierce and kind.

She's loyal and lovely,
sexy and wise.

And there is not a day
that passes,
I am not grateful
to have this phenomenal woman
in my life.

Facts 2

Treat her like a queen,
and you will live
a life of royalty.

Exactly What Happened

We found each other
one day
without even trying,
and though some
might call this fate,
we call it
exactly what happened.

The Lonely Crowd

I discovered
my loneliness
had nothing to do
with how many people
I was around,
but whether or not
I was around you.

Question & Answer

"How can you still love me
after all these years?"

"Because I fell in love
with your soul, my dear,
and your soul is timeless."

The Silence of Love

There is nothing quite like
holding you in the quiet,
listening to the rain
as it falls,
each drop
an echo,
a word spoken
and not spoken
between us.

There is nothing quite like
letting our souls rest
in the silence of love.

Shipwrecked

She came into my life
like a wave
stolen from the ocean;

She crowned me
with her kisses,
and rocked me
in her waters
until I loved
the sea.

She turned me
into a sailor,
unafraid to drown
in the name of love.

Love

is knowing
you can be
vulnerable,
and it
will not
be taken
advantage of.

When She Loves,
She Loves Forever

You and I,
love,
are forged
of diamonds,
blood,
and a fire
that will
never fade
from this
earth.

Just the Thought of You

I crave your body
against mine
like a hunger
born of wind and tide;

Without you,
I am like a child
stranded
on a deserted island
with nothing
but the sea and stars
to keep me company;

I crave the touch
of your skin
and the sound
of your voice
like a siren
singing
from
a distant shore.

I crave your laughter
like ripe fruits
that hang from a tree,
tempting me
to touch your forbidden heart,
and you wonder
why you leave me trembling
at just the thought
of you.

There is Beauty

in all the small things you give me;

There is magic in your kisses,
and miracles in your laughter;

And I admit this to you, my love,
so that you know
why I never grow tired
of this life we've made together
that is constantly
changing,
and always being reborn
in the ocean of your smile.

Truth

She is rare
because
she's real.

To be continued...

About the Author:

Mark Anthony is a bestselling poet who has written, "The Beautiful Truth," and "The Beautiful Life."

He is married to the woman of his dreams, and continues to live the life he's always wanted by being bold, and following his heart.

You can follow him on Instagram:

@markanthonypoet

& on Twitter:

@markanthon1

Printed in Great Britain
by Amazon